# Rubiks cube solving method of beginners

## Rubiks Cube Solution

L. Scales

# Contents

# Introduction

The rubiks cube was invented by the Hungarian Erno Rubik in 1974. It is loved by millions of people worldwide. It's popularity spread worldwide in the 1980s. Since the invention of the rubiks cube there has been more than 350,000,000 of them sold.

As low as one percent of people worldwide can solve the rubiks cube. Because of this and the rubiks cube popularity there will obviously be a huge number of individuals who seek to solve the cube. In the 1980s there wasn't as many opportunities to learn to solve the cube as there is today. There were extremely few books that taught to solve the cube and there was no internet access. However today there are a lot of books on this subject along with use of the internet where websites and You Tube videos can be found on this subject. Over the years many new rubiks cube solving methods have been introduced. The Long layer method is the method I recommend for beginners. Once you can solve the rubiks cube easily, naturally you will desire to solve it faster. In order to achieve this you will need to learn a much faster solving method. This will be a more advanced solving method which is one that solves the cube in a lot less moves. This will obviously lead to faster solving times. These more advanced solving methods are more complicated to learn than the beginners method. You may be talented enough to eventually produce solves under a minute. Individuals who can produce extremely fast solves of the cube are referred to as speedcubers. I would class a speedcuber as someone who can produce consistent solves of the cube under 30 seconds. Opinions do vary on this particular issue. Many speedcubers often go on to take part in major rubiks cube speedcubing competitions that are held all over the world. At the first Rubiks Cube World championships in 1982 the world record was broken by Minn Thai. He recorded a time of 22.95 seconds. Today the world record stands at a staggering time of 4.90 seconds by Lucas Etter. The main reasons for such a faster world record today is because the solving methods are of a lot less moves and carried out by finger pushes which are a lot faster than hand turns. There are about 30 individuals who have broken the speedcubing world record. These such individuals have become great speedcubing personalities. You can find a lot of information on the web about these characters. Today there are a lot of rubiks cube forums on the web. At them you are able to take part in discussions, ask questions and get advice. In this book I teach the Long layer method which is the easiest method for beginners. My tutorial also teaches you move notation and how the cube is made up. This book covers other rubiks cube related topics such as the names and brief descriptions of other learning methods. It covers speedcubing and discusses top speedcubers. You can get information about major speedcubing competitions and achievements. I also mention some speedcubing world records that have been broken. Furthermore I give you information about top rubiks cube forums and websites that you can visit. I decided to write this book to give rubiks cube lovers insights into every rubiks cube related activity. I have included the most crucial information in these chapters subjects to entertain the reader as much as possible. Read on and enjoy and learn.

# About the Author

L. Scales is one of the world's best tutors of the 3x3 rubiks cube. In 2009 he began making speedcubing videos and uploaded a lot of them to You Tube. Some of his speedcubing videos show his solves below 20 seconds. By March 2012 he began making rubiks cube tutorial videos. He trained at this for several months to become one of the world's top teachers of the 3x3 rubiks cube. His tutorials are designed to teach the beginners of the 3x3 rubiks cube and are designed in a way to help learners overcome the difficulties they may have experienced in other rubiks cube tutorials. His tutorial in this book is a written tutorial with diagrams illustrating the positions. His aim is to make the tutorial as easy, straightforward and enjoyable as possible.

# Chapter 1

# Learning
# The Rubiks Cube

The rubiks cube is made of 6 sides which are R=Right, L=Left, U=Upper, D=Downer, F=Face, B=Back. In rubiks cube notation if you read R, this would mean to turn the Right side a quarter turn clockwise. If you read R' this would mean to turn the Right side a quarter turn anti-clockwise. If you read R2, this would mean to turn the Right side in either direction 2 quarter turns. If you turned the R file in any direction 4 quarter turns, you would end up in the same position from where you started. If you read D' this would mean to turn the Downer side a quarter turn anticlockwise. If you read U, this would mean to turn the Upper clockwise a quarter turn. The rubiks cube is made up of 3 layers which are the first layer, the middle layer and the last layer. There are 3 different pieces that make up a rubiks cube. Firstly there are in all 8 corner pieces. Each corner piece consists of 3 different coloured stickers. Secondly there are in all 12 edge pieces. Each edge piece consists of 2 different coloured stickers. The edge pieces are located between the corner pieces. Thirdly there are 6 centre pieces. Each centre piece consists of a single sticker. The centre piece is the middle piece on each side. The centre pieces can't move at all they are fully stationary which means all the other same colours as the centre colour must be placed on the same side with that centre.

Now you want to get started learning the rubiks cube. As a beginner you would be wise choosing the easiest method of solving the rubiks cube. This tutorial will teach you to solve the rubiks cube using The Long Layer Method. This is the easiest learning method and it is the one I first learnt. After you've learnt this method you may decide you want to learn more advanced solving methods. This will give you step by step instructions including diagrams illustrating the positions. When referring to the moves of the cube I will not be using the commonly used algorithms. Instead I will state the name of the side to move. For example instead of stating R, I will just say Right. When an anticlockwise move is made I will state anticlockwise. So instead of stating R', I will just state Right anticlockwise. When I state Face, it means to turn the Face one quarter turn clockwise. When I state Face anticlockwise, it means to turn the Face one quarter turn anticlockwise. If I stated Downer twice, it means to turn the Downer twice. If you turned the Downer twice in either the clockwise or anti clockwise position you would still end up at the same point. Therefore if you turn any side twice it doesn't matter whether you play it in the clockwise or anticlockwise position. I prefer to teach using these move descriptions because it's a lot simpler and also because a lot of people don't like algorithms. You may be wondering how long it will take you to master the rubiks cube. Well this will depend mainly on two points. Firstly it will depend upon your natural learning ability for solving the rubiks cube. Secondly it will depend upon the amount of time and effort you dedicate to this tutorial. Learning the rubiks cube can be 5

very enjoyable but it can also be frustrating for some people. If you begin to feel frustrated whilst learning the rubiks cube then just take a rest. If you want to achieve anything in this world, you're going to need patience. I firmly believe most people could the rubiks cube within a few days if they applied their selves to this tutorial for at least an hour per day. You have plenty of detailed instructions with well illustrated diagrams to learn very well from this tutorial.

# Chapter 2

# **Move Notation**

B efore you learn to solve the rubiks cube it is advisable to learn the move notations. Move notation is the symbol that signifies the movement of a particular side of the cube. To begin with you will learn all the sides of the cube.

F = Front

The Front is the side of the cube that faces you.

B = Back

The Back is the side opposite the front.

U = Upper

The Upper is the side at the top of the cube.

D = Down

The Down is the side at the bottom of the cube or the side that's opposite the top of the cube.

L = Left

The Left is the side on the left of the front.

R = Right
The Right is the side on the right of the front.

f = Front two layers
These Front two layers are the side facing you and the layer after it which is the middle layer.

b = Back two layers
These Back two layers are the side opposite the front and the layer after it which is the middle layer.

u = Up two layers
These Up two layers are the side at the top and the layer after it which is the middle layer.

d = Down two layers
These Down two layers are the side at the bottom and the layer after it which is the middle layer.

l = Left two layers
These Left two layers are the side on the left of the front and the layer after it which is the middle layer.

r = Right two layers
These Right two layers are the side on the right of the front and the layer after it which is the middle layer.

x = (rotate) means to rotate the whole cube on R.

y = (rotate) means to rotate the whole cube on U.

z = means to rotate the whole cube on F.

When the symbol (') follows a letter, it means you must turn that side in the anti – clockwise direction.

For example U' means to turn the upper side one quarter turn in the anti- clockwise direction.

If a letter is written without a symbol, it means you must turn that side in the clockwise direction.

Therefore U means to turn the upper side one quarter turn in the clockwise direction.

A letter followed by a 2 or a small 2 that's not touching the line means to turn that side two quarter turns or an 180 degree turn.

The x, y, and z are used to indicate that the whole cube should be turned about one of its axes , corresponding to R, U, and F turns respectively.

If x, y, and z are primed, it means that the cube must be rotated in the opposite direction.

When they are squared, it means the cube must be rotated 180 degrees.

For methods that use middle – layer turns (particularly corners – first methods) there is "MES" extension to the notation where letters M,E and S denote middle layer turns. These notations were used in Marc Waterman's Algorithm.

M = Middle

This Middle layer is the layer between L and R.

E = Equator

This Equator layer is the layer between U and D.

S = Standing

This Standing layer is the layer between F and B.

Many cube solvers have solved the cube using these move notations.

Algorithms are a sequence of moves.

# Chapter 3

# **The Long Layer Method**

T here are 7 (seven) stages needed to complete to solve the cube using this method. These seven stages are to

1) Get a cross on the top layer

2) Place the corners correctly in the top layer

3) Place the edges in the middle layer

4) Get the last layer cross

5) Match up the cross edge colours

6) Position the corners correctly in the last layer

7) Solve the corners in the last layer

In this tutorial you can choose to either use the algorithms I've provided or just simply play the moves I mention. I will firstly state the algorithm required to solve each stage and then I will state the moves of that algorithm that need to be played. I will show you the original position before the piece is solved and then the position after the piece has been solved.

## Get the first layer cross

I will begin by solving the white layer. So firstly I must turn the white centre to the top. The white and orange edge and the white and green edge are already correctly placed in the top layer but you are only able to see their white stickers on the top layer. I know they are correctly placed because their edge colours are matching up with the centre colours their next to. For a piece to be correctly placed its sticker colours must match up with the centre colours their next to. On the Right side below the blue centre there is a red sticker of an edge piece as shown in Diagram 1.

The bottom of this edge piece has a white sticker. I need to place this white and red stickered edge piece on the top layer to match up with the other white stickers. When this white and red stickered edge is on the top layer its sticker colours must match the centre colours their next to. You will notice there is a red centre on the

Front. I can first match up the edges red sticker with the red centre by playing the following move.

D' = Downer side anticlockwise.

Now you can see the edges red sticker has been matched up with the red centre as shown in Diagram 2.

This matched up red edge piece has a white sticker at the bottom of the edge piece. I am now able to match this edges white sticker up with the white centre at the top of the cube by playing the following move.

F2 = two clockwise turns of the Front side.

After I play these moves you can now see the white and red edge piece has been correctly place in the top layer as shown in Diagram 3.

You can see a white and blue edge on the top layer wrongly placed between the white and blue centres. This edge piece must be placed correctly between the white and blue centres. In order to correctly place the white and blue edge piece in the top layer I must first play the following move.

R' = Right side anticlockwise.

This move gets the white and blue edge to the middle layer nearest to me. Now you can see this white and blue edge has moved where I want it in the middle layer as shown in Diagram 4.

In the above diagram the yellow and red edge piece can be seen in the top layer between the white and blue centres. Therefore I now need to place the white and blue edge in the position of the yellow and red edge piece. In order to do this I must first play the following move.

U = Upper side clockwise.

Now you can see that the yellow and red edge piece has moved to Front layer. The white and blue edge piece can now be moved to the position of the yellow and red edge piece as shown in Diagram 5.

Now I must play the following move.

F'= Face side anticlockwise.

This brings the white and blue edge in the position of the yellow and red edge piece. Now you can see the white and blue edge piece has moved to the top layer as shown in Diagram 6.

From the above position all the cross edge colours of the top white cross can now be matched up with their centre colours beneath them by playing the following move.

U'= Upper side anticlockwise.

Now you can see that the top white crosses edge colours are all matched up with their centre colours beneath them as shown in Diagram 7.

## Place the corners

From the above position you can see the first layer cross has now been solved. The next task is to correctly place all the corners pieces in the first layer. Because all the white stickers belong on the top layer I know that any corner piece with a white sticker must belong on this top layer. I will firstly place the red, white and blue corner in the top layer. The red, white and blue corner is out of view. I must now bring this corner piece into view by playing the following move.

D2 = Downer side two clockwise turns.

Now you can see this corner pieces red and white sticker has been brought into view and is positioned below the red centre on the right hand side as shown in Diagram 8.

From the above position the bottom sticker colour of this red and white corner piece is blue. Because this corner piece has red, white and blue stickers it means it must be placed between the red white and blue centres. Therefore this corner piece must be placed above the red centre in the top right hand corner position.

This top right hand corner must be turned down to place the white, blue and red corner piece in its position. This top right hand corner can be turned down in 2 different ways. The first way it can be turned down is by playing the following move.

F = Front side clockwise.

Now you can see the new position as shown in Diagram 9.

The other way the top right hand corner in Diagram 8 can be turned down is by playing the following move.

R' = Right side anticlockwise.

Now you can see the new position as shown in Diagram 10.

From this position I am able to join up the corner into position by playing the following move.

D' = Downer side anticlockwise.

You can now see that the red, white and blue corner piece is now placed into the correct position as shown in

Diagram 11.

I then play the following move.

R = Right side clockwise.

To turn the white stickers on the top layer as shown in Diagram 12.

From the above position an orange and blue stickered corner is seen below the red centre on the right hand

side. I will next place this orange and blue corner in the top layer. The bottom sticker colour of this corner is white. I need to place this corner between the orange, white and blue centres. So I must firstly turn the cube around to bring the orange and blue centres into view. After this I then play the move.

D = Downer side clockwise.

This places the corner between the orange and blue centres as shown Diagram 13.

Before I can place this corner correctly in the top layer I must firstly turn up its white sticker. In other words I must make sure its white sticker is no longer positioned at the bottom of the cube. In order to do this I must firstly play the move.

F = Front side clockwise.

Now the corner is positioned below the blue centre at the left hand side. The corners white sticker is out of view and its white sticker is no longer on the bottom but it is facing up at the side of the orange sticker. You are only able to see the corners orange sticker as shown in Diagram 14.

I then play the move.

D2 = Downer side 2 turns clockwise.

This brings the corners white sticker into view positioned below the orange centre on the right hand side as shown in Diagram 15.

I must then play the move

F' = Front anticlockwise

This brings the white stickers back on the top layer as shown in Diagram 16.

In order to now place the orange, white and blue corner in the top layer I must first position it up by playing the move.

D' = Downer side anticlockwise.

As shown in Diagram 17.

To enable me to now place the corner I play the

move F = Front clockwise.

As shown in Diagram 18.

In order to join up the corner I play the move.

D = Downer clockwise.

As shown in Diagram 19.

I finally turn the white stickers to the top layer by playing the move.

F' = Front anticlockwise.

As shown in Diagram 20.

I will now place the red, white and green corner in the top layer. This corner must be placed between the red, white and green centres because they're the same colours as the corners stickers. Therefore I must firstly turn the cube around to bring the red and green centres into view as shown in Diagram 21.

From the above position below the green centre on the right hand side you can see the green and white sticker of a corner piece. The sticker on the bottom of this corner is red. Before I can place this corner in the top layer I must first turn down the top corner by playing the move.

R' = Right anticlockwise.

As shown in Diagram 22.

I can now join up the corner by playing the move.

D' = Downer anticlockwise.

As shown in Diagram 23.

Then lastly I must bring the white stickers to the top layer by playing the move.

R = Right clockwise.

As shown in Diagram 24.

I will now place the last corner in the top layer which is the orange, white and green corner. This corner must be placed between the orange, white and green centres because they're the same colours as the corners stickers. Therefore I must firstly turn the cube around to bring the orange and green centres into view as shown in Diagram 25.

From the above position below the green centre on the right hand side a green corner sticker can be seen. The other sticker colours of this corner piece are orange and white. The white sticker of this corner is on the bottom. I must turn up this bottom white corner sticker before I can correctly place it on the top layer. So firstly I must place the corner between the orange and green centres by playing the move.

D' = Downer anticlockwise.

As shown in diagram 26.

I then turn up the corners bottom white sticker by playing the move.

F = Front clockwise.

As shown in Diagram 27.

In the above position the corners white sticker is now facing upwards but is out of view. I then bring the corners white sticker into view by playing the move.

D2 = Downer side two turns.

The corners white sticker is now visible below the green centre on the right hand side as shown in Diagram 28.

Next I turn the white stickers back to the top layer by playing the move.

F' = Front side anticlockwise as shown in Diagram 29.

I am now able to position up the white stickered corner piece to allow me to place it on the top layer by playing the move.

D' = Downer anticlockwise.

As shown in Diagram 30.

To enable me to join up my white stickered corner in the top layer I play the move.

F = Front clockwise.

As shown in Diagram 31.

I then join up the corner with the other white stickers by playing the move.

D = Downer clockwise.

As shown in Diagram 32.

Finally I bring the white stickers to the top layer by playing the move.

F' = Face anticlockwise.

As shown in Diagram 33.

Now you can see the top layer has been solved your next task is to solve the middle layer.

## Place the middle edges

You need to correctly place 4 edge pieces in order to solve the middle layer. All the white stickers are now on the top layer. All the yellow stickers belong on the bottom layer because that layer has a yellow centre. This means that all the edge pieces in the middle layer can't have either a white or yellow sticker on them when the cube has been fully solved. Therefore when I find an edge piece which has neither a white or yellow sticker on it then I know it must belong in the middle layer. A red and green edge sticker can be seen on the bottom as shown in Diagram 34.

This edge must be placed between the red and green centres because they're the same colours as the edges colours. To correctly place the red and green edge in the middle layer I must first correctly position it up. To do this you must first look at the colour at the bottom of the edge piece which is green. This means that I must turn this bottom green edge sticker opposite the green centre. To do this I must play the move.

D2 = Downer side two turns.

Now you can see the bottom green edge sticker is now faced opposite the green centre.

As shown in Diagram 35.

Because the edges other colour is red it means that I must now turn the red centre in front of me as shown in Diagram 36.

Assuming that the red stickers are the Front of my cube, in order to now correctly place the red and green edge into the middle layer I must play the moves.

L  D'  L'  D'  F'  D  F  =  Left clockwise, Downer anticlockwise, Left anticlockwise, Downer anticlockwise, Face anticlockwise, Downer clockwise, Face clockwise.

Now you can see the red and green edge piece is correctly placed in the middle layer.

As shown in Diagram 37.

In the next diagram an orange sticker of an edge piece can be seen on the bottom layer positioned opposite the orange centre. The other sticker on this edge is green. Therefore as I already have the bottom orange edge sticker facing opposite the orange centre I know it is correctly positioned to enable me to place it between the orange and green centre pieces as shown in Diagram 38.

Because this edge with the bottom orange sticker other colour is green it means I must now turn the green centre in front of me as shown in Diagram 39.

Assuming that the green stickers are the Front of my cube, in order to now correctly place the orange and green edge I must keep the green centre in front of me and play the moves.

L D' L' D' F' D F = Left, Downer anticlockwise, Left anticlockwise, Downer anticlockwise, Face anticlockwise, Downer clockwise, Face.

Now you can see the orange and green edge has been correctly placed as shown in Diagram 40.

If you have an incorrectly placed edge piece in the middle layer it must first be taken out in order to be accurately placed. The orange and blue edge is incorrectly placed in the middle layer as shown in Diagram 41.

In order to take out an incorrectly placed edge piece in the middle layer you must keep the incorrect edge at the Front left hand side of your cube. Assuming the blue stickers are my Face then you will see that the orange and blue edge is correctly positioned to be taken out. To now remove this incorrectly placed orange and blue edge I must play the moves.

L D' L' D' F' D  F = Left, Downer anticlockwise, Left anticlockwise, Downer anticlockwise, Face anticlockwise, Downer, Face.

You will notice that the incorrectly placed orange and blue edge has now moved from the middle layer to the bottom layer. The orange sticker of this orange and blue edge is out of view but its blue sticker can be seen. Opposite to this blue sticker you can see a red and blue edge piece.

As shown in Diagram 42

I will decide to firstly place this red and blue edge piece correctly in the middle layer. I must then firstly position this red and blue edge piece by turning its bottom blue sticker opposite the blue centre by playing the move.

D' = Downer anticlockwise.

As shown in Diagram 43.

This bottom blue sticker is on an edge piece that has a red colour on it which means I must next turn the red centre in front of me. In order to now place the edge piece in the middle layer I must keep this red centre in front of me. Assuming that the red stickers are at the Front of the cube I must now play the moves.

R' D R D F D' F' = Right anticlockwise, Downer clockwise, Right clockwise, Downer clockwise, Face clockwise, Downer anticlockwise, Face anticlockwise.

You can now see that the red and blue edge has now been correctly placed in the middle layer as shown in Diagram 44.

I will now proceed to place the last edge in the middle layer. This last middle edge piece is the orange and blue stickered edge as shown in Diagram 45.

As you now know that before placing this orange and blue edge piece in the middle layer I must firstly position it up by placing its bottom blue sticker opposite the blue centre. I achieve this by playing the move.

D2 = Downer side two turns.

I also bring the orange and blue centres into view.

As shown in Diagram 46.

Because the edges other colour is orange it means I must now turn the orange centre in front of me. In order to now place the edge I must keep the orange centre as my Front and play the moves.

L D' L' D' F' D F = Left clockwise, Downer anticlockwise, Left anticlockwise, Downer anticlockwise, Face anticlockwise, Downer clockwise, Face clockwise.

Now you can see the orange and blue edge has been correctly placed as shown in Diagram 47.

As you can see I have now successfully solved the first 2 layers of the rubiks cube. My next goal is to solve the last layer. So the first thing I need to do is to turn the rubiks cube upside down causing the white stickers to be on the bottom and the yellow centre on the top as shown in Diagram 48.

## Get the last layer cross

When I'm getting my cross I don't need to worry about whether there are any yellow corner stickers or not on the last layer. I only need to worry about the yellow edge stickers on the last layer.

The first stage of solving the last layer is to get a cross. Because I have a yellow centre on my last layer it means my cross must be a yellow one. This means I need to place all the 4 yellow edge stickers on the last layer which with the yellow centre will form a cross. To get a cross I will need to play either one, two, or three set of moves. It solely depends on the how many yellow edge stickers I already have on this last layer. You need to learn all the 3 stages. Firstly I will naturally start from a situation where I have no yellow edge stickers on the last layer as is the situation from diagram 48.

In diagram 48 I have the red stickers as my Front and to start to get my cross I must play the moves.

F R U R' U' F' = Front clockwise, Right clockwise, Upper clockwise, Right anticlockwise, Upper anticlockwise, Front anticlockwise.

Now you can see I now have 2 yellow edge stickers on the top layer as shown in Diagram 49.

If you imagine that all the last layer edge places are the points of a compass it means I must position these 2 yellow edge stickers in the North West position before playing the next set of moves to get my cross.

As shown in Diagram 50.

From the above position I must now play exactly the same moves I played for the first stage for the cross in order to complete this second stage. Therefore these moves to now play again are F R U R' U' F' = Front clockwise, Right clockwise, Upper clockwise, Right anticlockwise, Upper anticlockwise, Front anticlockwise.

You can see that I am now left with a yellow line as shown in Diagram 51.

I must now correctly position this yellow line before I can play the third stage for my cross. I must position this yellow line in a horizontal position. Remembering Red is my Face it means the yellow line must then be positioned as it is already seen. From here I will play the third stage for my cross which will be exactly the same moves I've previously played in the stages for the cross. When I play this third stage of the cross I will finally have the cross. I now play the moves.

F R U R' U' F'= Front clockwise, Right clockwise, Upper clockwise, Right anticlockwise, Upper anticlockwise, Front anticlockwise.

You can now see I have the yellow cross as Shown in Diagram 52.

## Match up the cross edge colours

Now that I have the cross I must next match up all the 4 cross edge colours with their centre colours below them. My cross edge colours are the sticker colours at the other side of the yellow edge stickers. You may be lucky enough to find that all the cross edge colours are already matching up with their centre colours below them. You will always have at least 2 cross edge colours that match up with their centre colours below them. In most cases you will have 2 cross edge colours that match up with their centre colours below them. Any 2 cross edge colours that match up with their centre colours below them fall into 2 categories. Firstly these matching edge colours can be opposite colours. For example the blue and the green cross edge colours or the red and the orange cross edge colours. Secondly these matching edge colours can be near colours. For example like the red and the green cross edge colours as shown in Diagram 53.

You will need to learn how to match up all the cross edge colours in both situations. In order to also match up the blue and orange cross edge colours I must firstly turn the cube around to bring the orange and blue centres into view and I must keep one of the non matching cross edge colours in front of me and the other one on the right hand side as shown in Diagram 54.

You can see that I need to swap the orange and blue cross edge colours around in order for them to match their centre colours below them. I have the orange centre as my Face and the blue cross edge colour is above the orange centre. The orange cross edge colour is on the right. To swap the orange and blue cross edge colours I must play the moves

R U2 R' U' R U' R' = Right clockwise, Upper twice, Right anticlockwise, Upper anticlockwise, Right clockwise, Upper anticlockwise, Right anticlockwise.

You can now see that all the 4 cross edge colours are now matching their centre colours below them as shown in Diagram 55.

When you have 2 opposite cross edge colours that match their centre colours below them you must play exactly the same moves as you would when you have 2 near cross edge colours that match their centre colours below them. When you have a situation where you have 2 opposite cross edge colours that match their centre colours below them you must hold one of the matching cross edge colours in front of you and play the moves.

R U2 R' U' R U' R' = Right clockwise, Upper twice, Right anticlockwise, Upper anticlockwise, Right clockwise, Upper anticlockwise, Right anticlockwise.

Next you must turn the Upper to match up the cross edge colours with their centre colours below them and you'll find you'll have 2 near cross edge colours that match their centre colours below them. You'll also have two near cross edge colours that don't match their centre colours below them which need to be swapped. I've already taught you how to solve two near cross edge colours that need to be swapped.

# Position the corners

My next task is to correctly position all the corners. In diagram 55 you can see that by luck I already have the yellow, orange, and blue stickered corner solved. If you had a red, white and blue stickered corner then you know for it to be correctly placed it must be placed between the red, white and blue centres. There are 3 possibilities concerning the positions of the corner pieces which are

1) No corner piece is correctly positioned.

2) One corner piece is correctly positioned.

3) All the corner pieces are correctly positioned.

Obviously you will only need to learn how to position your corners from the first 2 of these points. Before you start positioning the corner pieces you must choose a Face centre colour that must be kept in front of you while you are positioning the corner pieces. When there are no corner pieces in their correct positions you must try to get a corner in the correct position by playing the moves.

L' U R U' L U R' = Left anticlockwise, Upper clockwise, Right clockwise, Upper anticlockwise, Left clockwise, Upper clockwise, Right anticlockwise.

You must then turn the Upper to match up all the cross edge colours with their centre colours below them and then check to see if there are any corner pieces in the correct position. You may have a corner piece in the correct position but If there still isn't a corner piece in the correct position then you must keep the same centre colour in front of you and play exactly the same moves as before which were

L' U R U' L U R' = Left anticlockwise, Upper clockwise, Right clockwise, Upper anticlockwise, Left clockwise, Upper clockwise, Right anticlockwise and you will now definitely have a corner piece in the correct position. Once you have a corner piece in the correct position you must hold the cube so that this corner piece is on your Front in the top right hand corner position. Before I position my corners I find that in diagram 55 I already have the yellow, orange and blue stickered corner piece already in the correct position. This means I must now hold the cube so that this corner piece is in the Front top right hand corner position and I must keep the orange centre in front of me while I position the rest of the corner pieces. From this position I must now move the corner pieces by playing the moves

L' U R U' L U R' = Left anticlockwise, Upper clockwise, Right clockwise, Upper anticlockwise, Left clockwise, Upper clockwise, Right anticlockwise.

I must now turn the Upper to match up all the cross edge colours with their centre colours below them and I find my correctly positioned corner is still in the correct place and the three wrongly positioned corner pieces have moved places but are still in the wrong positions as shown in Diagram 56.

Sometimes you will have all the corner pieces in their correct positions at this stage. Because I still only have the same corner piece in the correct position it means I will have to play exactly the same moves again keeping the orange centre in front of me and the correct corner in the Front top right hand corner position. Once I played these same moves again as

L' U R U' L U R' = Left anticlockwise, Upper clockwise, Right clockwise, Upper anticlockwise, Left clockwise, Upper clockwise, Right anticlockwise.

I found that I now have all the 4 corner pieces in their correct positions as shown in Diagram 57.

The next stage will be your final stage to complete the rubiks cube. This next stage will be to solve the corners.

## Solve the corners

In order to solve these corners I need to get each corners yellow sticker to the top layer to match up with the rest of the yellow stickers. When each corner piece is solved you'll notice that the corners other sticker colours also match up with the other same colours on the cube. You must make sure the yellow centre is kept on top. Before I begin to solve these corners I need to choose a centre colour to keep in front of me as my Face while I solve all these corners. I will choose to keep the blue centre in front of me as my Face while I solve all the corners. Every corner must be positioned at the front top right hand corner before solving. I will decide to first solve the red, yellow and blue stickered corner since it is already correctly positioned in the front top right hand corner as shown in Diagram 58.

To solve the corners I only need to keep playing the same 4 moves and then after the fourth move I must check to see if the corners yellow sticker is on the top layer. You will have to play two sets of these 4 moves or four sets of these 4 moves to solve any corner piece. If I see the corners yellow sticker is on the top layer it means that I must stop because that corner is now solved. The cube will get a bit messed up while your solving these corners but it doesn't matter because all the colours will join up once you've solved all the corners. I will start solving this corner by playing the moves

R F' R' F = Right clockwise, Front anticlockwise, Right anticlockwise, Front clockwise.

I now check to see if the corners yellow sticker is on the top layer and I find it isn't as shown in Diagram 59.

Because the corners yellow sticker isn't on the top layer it means I must again play the same 4 moves again which are

R F' R' F = Right clockwise, Front anticlockwise, Right anticlockwise, Front clockwise.

I then check to see if the corners yellow sticker is on the top layer and I find that it now is as shown in Diagram 60.

This means this corner is now solved. I then now keep the same blue centre in front of me as my Face and then turn the Upper to bring any next unsolved corner to the front top right hand corner position to be solved as shown in Diagram 61.

From this position I then played the same 4 moves to solve this corner which are

R F' R' F = Right clockwise, Front anticlockwise, Right anticlockwise, Front clockwise.

I then checked for the corners yellow sticker and I found it wasn't on top and so I then played the same 4 moves again which are

R F' R' F = Right clockwise, Front anticlockwise, Right anticlockwise, Front clockwise.

And I saw the corners yellow sticker was now on the top layer as shown in Diagram 62.

From the above position I then made sure I still kept the blue centre in front of me and turned the Upper to bring the next and last unsolved corner to the front top right hand corner position to be solved as shown in Diagram 63.

I then played the 4 moves to solve this corner which are R F' R' F = Right clockwise, Front anticlockwise, Right anticlockwise, Front clockwise.

I then checked for the corners yellow sticker and I found it wasn't on the top layer and so I played the same 4 moves again as

R F' R' F = Right clockwise, Front anticlockwise, Right anticlockwise, Front clockwise.

and I found the corners yellow sticker was now on the top layer as shown in Diagram 64.

Now all the corners are solved you can notice how all the last layer edge colours are all matching up. It looks beautiful. All you need to do now is to fully solve the cube by playing the move

U2 = Upper side two turns

And congratulations you have now solved the rubiks cube as shown in Diagram 65.

# Chapter 4

# A brief look at learning methods to find on the web

Today there are numerous ways of solving the rubiks cube. All these solving methods have evolved over the last three decades. When deciding what solving methods to learn you must first consider your goal. You may just want to learn to solve the rubiks cube. Alternatively you may have already learned to solve the rubiks cube and now want to learn a faster solving method. The three most common learning methods of solving the rubiks cube are, The Long Layer method, the Fridrich method and the Lars Petrus method. The latter being the most advanced method. There are also a lot of other learning methods. There are hand written tutorials of the three main learning methods which are assisted by well illustrated diagrams. I would strongly recommend a beginner to learn The Long Layer method. This is the easiest of all the learning methods. This is the original method designed to solve the rubiks cube. It takes a maximum of 120 quarter turns of the cube to solve it by using The Long Layer method. There are seven stages needed to complete the cube using this method. These seven stages are to

1) Get a cross on the top layer

2) Place the corners correctly in the top layer

3) Place the edges correctly in the middle layer

4) Get a cross on the last layer

5) Solve the cross edge colours

6) Place the corners correctly

7) Solve the corners.

The first three of these stages are fairly straightforward but the rest of these stages will take more thinking about. This tutorial is designed to help learners overcome the difficulties they sometimes experience learning the rubiks cube. Well illustrated diagrams are included in this tutorial. This step by step tutorial thoroughly explains every situation in detail. The Lars Petrus method and the Fridrich method are advanced methods of solving the rubiks cube. These methods should only be learnt once a person has already learnt to solve the rubiks cube.

# The Lars Petrus Method

The rubiks cube will be solved in an average of 75 moves by using this method. It is a very complicated learning method. There are seven steps needed to complete the cube using this method which include:

1) Step 1-Build a 2x2x2 corner

2) Step 2-Expand to 2x2x3

3) Step 3-Twist the edges, you will either have 2,4,or 6 edges

4) Step 4-Finish 2 layers

5) Step 5-Position the corners

6) Step 6-Twist the corners

7) Step 7-Positon the edges

You can get help with block building tricks for steps 1, 2, and 4. There are also 13 example solutions you can practice.

# The Fridrich Method

This is the most advanced learning method of solving the rubiks cube. It is used by most of the world's top speedcubers. This method was invented in the early 1980s by a group of speedcubers who created the algorithms. It was put online in 1997 by Jessica Fridrich. This method of solving the rubiks cube consists of a maximum of 120 algorithms. The steps needed to solve the cube by this method are as follows.

# F2L–First 2 Layers

To solve the first 2 layers you must place a corner with a matching colour edge piece in a certain position. Next you must play the correct sequences of moves to join the corner and edge piece. Once they're joined with their colours matching up the corner will be at the top and the edge will be in the middle layer. There are 42 algorithms that need to be learnt in order to solve the first 2 layers. Once the first 2 layers have been completed the next step is to orientate the last layer.

# OLL – Orientate Last Layer

To orientate the last layer means to make all that last layer the same colour as its centre colour. For example if your last layer had a yellow centre then it would mean all the other sticker colours on that layer must also be made yellow. There are 58 algorithms that need to be learnt to carry out the OLL stage. The last and final stage is to permute the last layer.

# PLL – Permute Last Layer

To permute the last layer means to match up all the last layers side colours. Once this is done the rubiks cube will be completed. There are 13 algorithms that need to be learnt to carry out the PLL stage. Other advanced rubiks cube solving methods are the Waterman method and the Roux method. The Waterman method is carried out by solving the corners first. It is one of the most complex and optimized methods to learn and has many sequences that need to be mastered. The Roux method is a commonly used method by world class speedcubers. This is a last 6 edges rubiks cube solving method.

# Chapter 5

# **Speedcubing guide for beginners**

O nce an individual has learnt to solve the rubiks cube it is only natural for them to want to solve it faster.

## **Speedcubing**

Speedcubing is the art of solving the rubiks cube as fast as possible. There are also other twisty puzzles in which speedcubing is possible. Generally a rubiks cube solver would be considered to be a speedcuber if they could solve the cube within 30 seconds.

## **Algorithms**

Once you've learnt the move notation you'll be able to learn algorithms. Top class speed cubers solve the cube within 15 seconds. In order to carry out such fast solves of the cube many algorithms must be memorized. The more algorithms memorized means the less amount of moves are needed to solve the cube. Moves of the R = right file and the U = Upper file, are the easiest and quickest moves to carry out. Therefore algorithms containing the most R and U file will enable you to solve the cube as fast as possible. After lots of practice you will eventually be able to play these algorithms off by heart.

## Flexible rubiks cube

To enable speed cubing, one will need a flexible cube. Some brands of rubiks are very stiff, which slows down your moves enormously. These are very cheap rubiks cubes. Your rubik's will loosen up simply by using it. You can also loosen up your rubik's cube by lubricating it or by removing the centre piece caps and loosening the screws which in turn loosens the springs. This will result in a much more flexible cube that turns very easily. I f you decide to lubricate your cube I would strongly recommend you use silicon spray. Before lubricating your cube you should read an article on lubrication. There are many rubik's cube online specially designed for speed cubing.

## Finger Tricks

Learning finger tricks will enable you to speed solve a cube a lot faster. Finger tricks are a way of executing a certain combination of moves faster. There are some websites with videos that show you how to perform algorithms. A collection of videos found here on the following forums will help you to learn finger tricks.

(http://www.speedsolving.com/forum/showthread.
php?5248 – Help – thread – Finger – Tricks).

www.cubewhiz.com provides algorithms with videos.
This can give you an idea about how to execute
certain combinations of moves.

www.strangepuzzle.com hosts a lot of speedcubing
videos. These videos are really fast, but it can give
you some inspiration. After watching all these videos
for a while, you will probably start performing your
own tricks.

## Cube Speed solving methods

There are many methods to solve the rubik's cube.
Obviously a beginner is advised is advised to learn the
easiest and fastest method known as the Long layer
method. By using this method, you will solve the cube
in an average of 115 quarter turn moves. If you are
a serious speedcuber you will need to use a method
that solves the cube in much less moves. The Fridrich
method and the Lars Petrus method are two such
methods that do this. These two methods are used
by world class speedcubers. The Lars Petrus method
solves the cube in an average of 75 quarter turn moves.
The more commonly used Fridrich method solves the
cube in an average of 65 quarter turn moves. With a
bit of luck world class speedcubers have solved the
cube using the Fridrich method in as few as 35 quarter
turn moves. This is the main reason why some world
class speedcubers have been able to solve the cube

between 5 and 6 seconds. The world record today for speedsolving the cube stands at 5.24 seconds.

## Buying puzzles

Due to the immense desire for rubiks cubes many shops have appeared. These shops include:

http://thecubicle.us/ - This place sells various puzzles which are very popular amongst speedcubers. They also offer world wide shipping.

http://cubezz.com/ - They tend to have all the new cubes on sale very quickly. They also offer free shipping.

http://lightake.com/ - This site have lots of cubes that are regularly bought by speedcubers.

http://www.mefferts.com - They offer a large number of different and interesting puzzles. They don't especially focus on speedcubes.

## Big cubes

Big cubes refers to the 4x4 and 5x5 cubes. You can learn to solve these big cubes at sites such as:

http://www.speedcubing.com/chris/4 - solution.html and

http://www.bigcubes.com

## How to solve the cube fast

To enable you to produce your fastest solves of the cube you mustn't rush. You must learn to slow down, look ahead and concentrate. You must also put in plenty of hard practice. There are speedcubing tutorial videos at You Tube that you will find helpful to improve your speedcubing times.

## Official Speedcubing world records

All official world records for fast solves of the cube achieved at competitions can be found here:

http://www.worldcubeassociation.org/results/index.php

All unofficial world records for fast solves of the cube can be found here:

http://www.speedcubing.com/records

Frequently asked questions
For these questions please visit this link

http://www.speedsolving.com/forum/faq.php

The page containing the most links to speedcubing is found here:

http://speedcubing.com/links.html

How to Guides

This is a link to the How – To section, which includes various tutorials and guides.

http://www.speedcubing.com/forum/forumdisplay.php?f=18

The link to the wiki page for the popular Layer by Layer beginners method is at

http://www.speedsolving.com/wiki/index.php/Layer     -
by - layer

# Chapter 6

# Improving Your Speedcubing Times

O nce an individual has learnt to solve the rubiks cube it is only natural for them to want to solve it faster. Practising more will help to achieve this. Apart from practice there are two other main ways to produce faster solving times. These include learning to solve the cube in less moves and learning to carry out moves of the cube by quick finger pushes. The Fridrich method consists of 120 algorithms which once mastered enables the cuber to solve the cube in an average of 65 moves. Finger pushes on the cube are carried out much faster than by moves carried out by turns of the hand. The fast finger pushes cuts out the time delay from turns of the hand. You can also get help to cube faster by getting advice from speedcubers You can also watch speedcubing tutorials on the web which will give you more insights into speedcubing. Today there are numerous speedcubing videos on the web and also many finger pushing tutorials. I have found these tutorials very useful. Firstly you should watch the basic finger pushing tutorials and once mastered you can go on to watch the more advanced tutorials. There are a lot of both of these tutorials at You Tube. Rubiks cube world champion Felix Zemdegs hosts numerous finger pushing tutorials which are very popular. These finger skills are essential if a speedcuber wants to produce solves under 20 seconds. There's more algorithms being created and more advanced finger pushing tutorials being introduced all the time. With these continually increasing faster solving times are being produced and may be one day the rubiks cube solving world record will stand under 4.5.

# Chapter 7

# **Becoming A Speedcuber**

What is a speedcuber one may ask themselves. The simple answer to this question is different to different people. For some people a speedcuber is someone who can solve the cube under one minute. There are extremely few people who can solve the rubiks cube under one minute. Therefore I would consider them very good. A lot more people would consider a speedcuber to be able to solve the cube under 30 seconds. Everyone would definitely agree that any person who can solve the cube under 20 seconds is definitely a speedcuber. I would expect a speedcuber to be able to at least solve a cube at 3 moves per second. This speed is very fast. I first learned to solve the cube in 1982. After 3 months of practice I could solve the cube in 27 seconds. At that time the fastest speedcubers in the world were solving the cube in this same time as me. I at that time would have been considered a world class speedcuber. The rubiks cube solving method used in 1982 was called The long layer method. This method consisted of about 10 algorithms. The moves of the cube were carried out by hand turns. Using this method it would take a maximum of 120 quarter turns to solve the cube. As time progressed better solving methods were introduced enabling a cuber to solve the cube in less moves. This led to faster solving times. These faster solving times were improved further by using finger pushes. Finger pushes are carried out solely by the use of your fingers. World class speedcubers of today average about 5-6 turns per second when carrying out moves by finger pushes. Finger pushes are carried out on the Upper,Downer,Front and Back files. The Left and Right files need to be moved by hand turns. Finger pushes are carried out by using every finger excluding the smallest one. Even the thumbs can be used in finger pushing. Finger pushes are carried out by holding the cube with your thumbs and middle and wedding fingers. You must now make quick pushes with your index finger to carry out moves on the Upper,Front and Back files. To carry out moves on the Downer file you must hold the cube with your thumbs, middle and index fingers and push the Downer file with your wedding fingers. Apart from producing much faster solves by finger finger pushes it also looks a lot more cooler. The development of these speedcubing skills has led to world class speedcubers averaging solves under 15 seconds. If you're serious about becoming a speedcuber you must be dedicated to learning. You must practice a lot and I would advise you to do some research on the subject.

# Chapter 8

# Speedcubing World Records Under 20 Seconds

The first world record set for solving the rubiks cube under 20 seconds was achieved at the West German Championship 1982. This championship witnessed the German born Ronald Brinkmann produce a solve of 19.00 seconds.

This world record was then broken by Robert Pergyl of Czechoslovakia. He achieved this at the Czechoslovakian Championship 1982 by clocking 17.02 seconds.

There was a massive gap until the next Rubiks Cube World Championships which wasn't held until 2003. At this World Championships Dan Knights of the USA broke the rubiks cube world record with a solve in 16.71seconds.

In the same year Jesse Bonde of Denmark solved the rubikscubein16.53secondsatthesamechampionships in 2003. Japanese born Shotaro Makisumi is one of the biggest names in the history of the speedcubing world. This isn't surprising considering he's broken the world record five times for solving the rubiks cube. In the year 2004 Makisumi improved the current world record of 16.53 seconds down to 12.11 seconds.

He broke the world record for the first time at the Caltech Winter Competion 2004, by solving the cube in 15.07 seconds. He then went on to solve the rubiks cube in 14.76 seconds at this same competition breaking the world record again. Later on in the same year Makisumi competed at the Caltech Spring Competition. At this competition he broke his previous rubiks solving world record by clocking 13.89 seconds which was a new world record. He broke the world record again at this same competition by solving the cube in an amazing 12.11 seconds.

# Chapter 9

# Top Speedcubing Personalities

S ince the invention of the rubiks cube certain individuals have made a big impact solving the rubiks cube. These people will live long in people's memories. Although Minn Thai may not have been one of the fastest ever speedcubers, the fact that he won the first ever Rubiks Cube World Championships gives him a place in history. Furthermore he also broke the world record at this 1982 Rubiks Cube World Championships. However I have no knowledge of any rubiks cube related events since that he's been a part of.

## Tyson Mao

Tyson Mao was a world class speedcuber in 2005. He is mostly remembered for solving the rubiks cube blindfolded on CNN TV in front of millions of viewers. He competed in the 2005 Rubiks Cube World Championships. In 2005 he was averaging 15 second solves of the rubiks cube which was world class standard at that time. In 2006 he broke the blindfolded world record for solving the rubiks cube. Tyson Mao's fame increased even further by becoming the co founder and a current board member of the World Cube Association.

## Toby Mao

Although Toby Mao didn't achieve anything compared to other top speedcubers to be that memorable he did break the world record.

He achieved this in 2006 in a time of 10.48 seconds. He is easily remembered because he is Tyson Mao's brother.

## Thiabald Jacquinot

Thiabald Jacquinot has certainly made his place in history by being the first person to solve the rubiks cube under 10 seconds. He clocked 9.86 seconds at the Spanish Open 2007 to achieve this.

## Felix Zemdegs

Felix Zemdegs is by far the most memorable figure in the history of the speedcubing world. He has set untold records. Firstly Felix Zemdegs is the youngest person to break the world record for solving the rubiks cube. In the year 2010 at the age of 14 Felix set a world record by solving the rubiks cube in 6.77 seconds. He has gone on to break his own world record five times. He has held the world record for the fastest rubiks cube solve six times, which is more times than anyone in history. He has also won the most speedcubing competitions than anyone else. He has set world records for the fastest solves for the 3x3, 4x4, and 5x5 rubiks cube solves. Further to this he has also set a world record for the 7x7 average rubiks cube solves and set a world record for the rubiks cube one handed solve. He has the fastest Rubiks Cube World Championship winning time which he achieved in the 2013 World Championships. He won this World Championships in 8.18 seconds.

## Matts Valk

Matts Valk must obviously be in all our minds as he is now the world record holder for solving the rubiks cube. His speedcubing world record stands at 5.55 seconds.

# Chapter 10

# World's First Rubiks Cube Competition

The first Rubiks Cube World Championships was held in Hungary Budapest 1982. 19 countries participated in this competition. These countries included Austria, Belgium, Bulgaria, Canada, Czechoslovakia, Finland, France, Great Britain, Holland, Hungary, Italy, Japan, Peru, Poland, Portugal, Sweden, United States, West Germany and Yugoslavia. The competition rules differed a lot in comparison of today. Each comp had to solve the cube three times. The fastest of each competitor three solves was used to decide the winner of the competition. The moves of the rubik's cube weren't carried out by finger pushes as they are in this modern day. Instead moves were carried out by hand turns. The solving method used by the competitors was called The Long Layer Method. This was the original method of solving the rubiks cube. Before solving the rubiks cube each competitor was given the privilege of 15 seconds to view the cube. At this contest the cubes were shuffled by computer and then brought on stage in a sealed suit case. Then the rubiks cube was placed on a small pad. The competitor would then view the cube for 15 seconds which started as soon as they picked up the cube which started the clock. Within 15 seconds the competitor had to place the cube back down. Now the competitor was ready to solve the cube. The clock would immediately start as soon as the cube to be solved was picked up. When the competitor finished their solve of the cube they would then place the cube back down which automatically stopped the timer. If during their solve they were misfortunate enough for their cube to dissemble, then they were given another chance to solve the cube. However if the cube dissembled a second time during their solve of the cube, then they weren't given another chance. My only criticism of this competition is that the competition failed to supply the competitors of flexible rubiks cubes. I'm aware that this didn't put any competitor at any disadvantage considering they all used the same non flexible rubiks cubes. It would be more easier for the competitors to have been supplied decent rubiks cubes and their times would have been faster. The completion was won by 16 year old Minn Thai. He produced the fastest solve at this competition of 22.95 seconds breaking the world record.

Made in the USA
San Bernardino, CA
22 May 2017